Benjamin Franklin

Leni Donlan

Chicago, Illinois

Customer Service: **888-454-2279**

Visit our website at **www.raintreelibrary.com**

Designed by Kimberly R. Miracle and Betsy Wernert
Photo Research by Tracy Cummins
Map on page 29 by Mapping Specialists
Printed in China by Leo Paper Group

12 11 10 09 08
10 9 8 7 6 5 4 3 2 1

Library of Congress Cataloging-in-Publication Data
Donlan, Leni.
  A life well lived : Benjamin Franklin / Leni Donlan.
     p. cm. -- (American history through primary sources)
  Includes bibliographical references and index.
  ISBN-13: 978-1-4109-2698-2 (hardcover)
  ISBN-13: 978-1-4109-2709-5 (pbk.)
 1. Franklin, Benjamin, 1706-1790--Juvenile literature. 2. Statesmen--United States--Biography--Juvenile literature. 3. Scientists--United States--Biography--Juvenile literature. 4. Inventors--United States--Biography--Juvenile literature. 5. Printers--United States--Biography--Juvenile literature. I. Title. II. Title: Ben Franklin.
  E302.6.F8D595 2008
  973.3092--dc22
  [B]
                            2007005909

Acknowledgments
The author and publisher are grateful to the following for permission to reproduce copyright material: Library of Congress Prints and Photographs Division **pp 4-5, 11 bottom, 14, 16, 18, 19, 20, 21, 22, 23, 24–25, 26**; Library of Congress Geography and Map Division **pp. 6 top, 24 top**; Library of Congress Manuscript Division **pp. 10, 11 top, 15, 17**; Getty Images **pp. 6** bottom (Kean Collection/ Archive Photos), **9** (MPI), **13** (Kean Collection); The Granger Collection **p. 12**; Dave G. Houser/Corbis **p. 27**.

Cover image of Ben Franklin portrait reproduced with the permission of Library of Congress Prints and Photographs Division.

The publishers would like to thank Nancy Harris for her assistance in preparing this book.

Every effort has been made to contact copyright holders of any material reproduced in this book. Any omissions will be rectified in subsequent printings if notice is given to the publishers.

Contents

Some words are printed in bold, **like this**. You can find out what they mean on page 30. You can also look in the box at the bottom of the

An Amazing American

Benjamin Franklin was an amazing man. He was an American. He was a printer and a writer. He was a scientist and an inventor. He was a musician. Ben was a **philosopher**. He was known for his ideas and thinking. Ben was also a **diplomat**. He was good at dealing with people.

Ben respected people. People in the American **Colonies** (see box) knew Ben. So did people in the countries of England and France. They all respected him. Ben thought people should be friendly to others. He said that people should be "enemy to none."

Ben was a great thinker. He felt free to do things his own way. Ben was hardworking. He liked to think about new ideas. He worked hard to make his world a better place.

Ben had big ideas about what the United States could be. His ideas helped shape the country. Ben's ideas still live today. He is one of the greatest people in U.S. history.

The Colonies

Before there was the United States, there were 13 colonies. England ruled them. These colonies later became the first states. (See map on page 29.)

colony	land belonging to or under the control of a nation that is far away
diplomat	person who is good at dealing with other people. Diplomats often work for the government (leaders) of a country.
philosopher	person known for ideas and thinking

Ben Franklin loved to read and write.

Ben's Childhood

This map was made in the 1700s. It shows how Boston might have looked when Ben was a boy.

This is the Franklin home in Boston, Massachusetts.

apprentice   person who is learning a job
resolve   decide

Ben was born on January 17, 1706. He was born in Boston, Massachusetts. He was one of seventeen children. Ben was the youngest son.

Young Ben liked to swim and fish in Boston Harbor. Ben invented ways to make swimming easier. He tied paddles to his hands and feet. He even tied a kite to his waist. This pulled him through the water!

Ben loved learning. He taught himself to read. He learned to write by studying the writing of others. Ben attended Boston Grammar School for two years.

Ben left school to work when he was ten years old. He worked for his father. He worked at his candle- and soap-making job. Ben's father hated to make him leave school. Ben did not want to work for his father.

When he was twelve, Ben went to work for his brother James. He worked at James's print shop. He became an **apprentice**. An apprentice is someone who is learning a new job.

Ben's words

"**Resolve** [decide] each morning to make the day a happy one."

Printer and Writer

Ben promised to work for James until he was 21 years old. In return, James gave Ben a place to sleep. He gave him food to eat. James taught Ben to be a printer.

Ben worked hard. He worked every day but Sunday. Ben became a very good printer.

Ben also worked hard at becoming a good writer. He wanted people to read his writing. But James would not print Ben's work. So, Ben tricked James.

Ben wrote **articles** (short writings) under a false name! He signed his writings with the name "Silence Dogood." Ben slipped the articles under the door of the print shop late at night.

James thought the articles by Silence Dogood were wonderful. He printed them in his newspaper.

When James found out about the trick, he was angry. Ben and James were now unhappy working together. Ben decided to run away.

Ben went to Philadelphia, Pennsylvania. He found a job in a print shop. Philadelphia was Ben's home for the rest of his life.

article short writing such as those printed in newspapers
printing press machine used to print newspapers and signs
seldom not often

"Anger is never without Reason, but **seldom** [not often] with a good One."

This was Ben Franklin's **printing press**.

His own business

Ben went to London, England, to learn more about printing. Ben then went home to Philadelphia. He started his own printing business.

Ben printed a newspaper. It was called the *Pennsylvania Gazette*. He wrote many of the **articles** (short writings) himself. He also printed an **almanac** (see box). He printed other things, too.

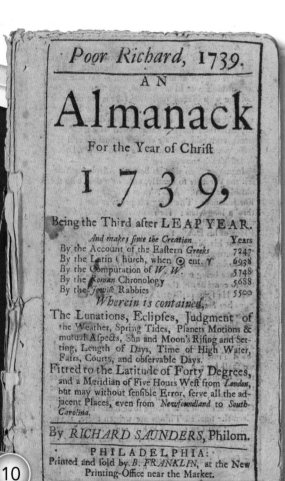

Poor Richard, 1739.

AN

Almanack

For the Year of Chrift

1739,

Being the Third after LEAP YEAR.

And makes fince the Creation Years
By the Account of the Eaftern *Greeks* 7247
By the Latin Church, when ☉ ent. ♈ 6938
By the Computation of *W. W.* 5748
By the *Roman* Chronology 5688
By the *Jewifh* Rabbies 5500

Wherein is contained,

The Lunations, Eclipfes, Judgment of the Weather, Spring Tides, Planets Motions & mutual Afpects, Sun and Moon's Rifing and Set-ting, Length of Days, Time of High Water, Fairs, Courts, and obfervable Days.

Fitted to the Latitude of Forty Degrees, and a Meridian of Five Hours Weft from *London,* but may without fenfible Error, ferve all the ad-jacent Places, even from *Newfoundland* to *South-Carolina.*

By RICHARD SAUNDERS, Philom.

PHILADELPHIA:
Printed and fold by *B. FRANKLIN,* at the New Printing-Office near the Market.

Almanacs

In the 1700s, most people did not own many books. They did own an almanac. An almanac shows the days, weeks, and months of the year. It **forecasts** the weather. People read it to find out what type of weather is expected. Almanacs also have recipes, jokes, and odd facts.

Ben wrote his almanac using a fake name. He used the name Richard Saunders. Ben called the almanac *Poor Richard's Almanac*. A new almanac came out every year for 25 years. It helped make Ben rich and famous.

almanac book printed once a year that includes a calendar and weather forecasts
forecast to tell what will happen at a later date (such as the weather)

Ben even printed money! Ben and a partner printed money for three states. They were Pennsylvania, New Jersey, and Delaware. The money was called "bills of credit." The U.S. government backed bills of credit. Slowly, people began to trust this "paper money."

Ben printed paper money. They were called bills of credit.

This shows Ben Franklin (center) and pictures from his writings.

Ben Settles Down

Ben decided it was time to settle down. He wanted to be serious about his life.

Ben married Deborah Read in 1730. Deborah was not like Ben. She could barely read or write. Still, they were happy together.

Ben opened a store next door to his print shop. Deborah loved working there. She was a good helper with Ben's businesses.

This picture shows Ben and Deborah Read. This was before they were married.

Ben's words

"Early to bed and early to rise makes a man healthy, wealthy, and wise."

smallpox   serious illness that causes skin rash, high fever, and sometimes death

This is Ben's daughter, Sarah. Her parents called her "Sally."

Ben had three children. He had two sons, William and Frances "Franky" Folger. Sadly, Franky died of **smallpox** when he was just four years old. Smallpox is a serious illness. Deborah and Ben had a daughter named Sarah. They called her Sally.

Ben and Deborah always missed little Franky. Sally was a joy to her father all his life. William and Ben loved one another. But they did not always agree about things.

Inventor and Scientist

Ben liked to solve problems. He became an inventor so he could solve problems. He became a scientist so he could understand the world.

Ben designed the Pennsylvania fireplace to solve a problem. People used fireplaces for heat. But most of the heat went up and out the **chimney**. Ben's fireplace gave off more heat. It also used less wood than a regular fireplace. Today, his invention is known as the Franklin stove.

Ben is watching his science tools. He is taking notes about what happens during a storm.

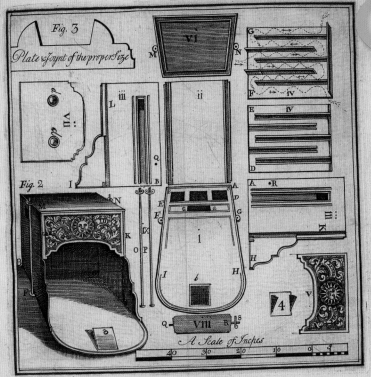

This is Ben's design for **bifocal** eyeglasses.

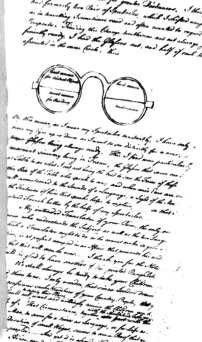

Ben's Franklin stove was a very important invention.

Ben solved another problem. He needed eyeglasses to see well. As he got older, Ben needed a second pair of glasses for reading. He did not like having to switch glasses. So Ben had the **lenses** cut in half. The lenses are the clear part that is looked through. He joined the tops of his everyday glasses to the bottoms of his reading glasses. These eyeglasses were called **bifocals**. (*Bi* means "two" and *focal* refers to "focus.")

15

Important discovery

In 1743 Ben started the American Philosophical Society. This was a group of men who met to share ideas. They shared ideas about science and other subjects.

Ben wanted to test his ideas about **electricity**. Electricity is a type of energy. Energy makes things work.

Ben wanted to know how electricity traveled. He studied **lightning**. Lightning flashes in a thunderstorm. Lightning has electrical power. Ben used a metal key attached to the string of a kite. The kite brought the key up closer to lightning. Ben wanted to see if the electrical power of lightning would pass through the metal key. He found that it did. This experiment showed how electricity traveled.

The story about Ben and the lightning storm is very famous.

armonica   instrument played by touching the edges of spinning glass bowls with wet fingers

Making music

Ben played the violin and the guitar. He used his understanding of science to build his own instrument. It was called the **armonica**. The armonica had spinning glass bowls. It was played by touching the edges of these bowls. It was a very popular instrument for many years.

Ben was very proud of the armonica. He said it meant more to him than his other inventions.

Public Servant

Ben also wanted to provide **services** that people needed. Services are groups such as fire departments.

Ben started a club called the Junto Club in 1727. They met to talk about the **issues** of the day. An issue is what is important at the time.

What issues do you think the Junto Club would talk about today?

Ben met a group of people in the club. He thought these people might want to help him. Ben began thinking about ways to improve his city.

Ben and his friends started a **volunteer** fire department. Volunteers work without being paid. Ben and his friends also worked to improve police services in their city. Philadelphia became a safer place to live.

Ben began working for the public. He worked for the good of others.

issue	what is important at the time, such as wars or public needs
opportunity	chance
service	group that works for the needs of the public, such as a police department
volunteer	person who provides a service without being paid

"We should be glad of an **opportunity** [chance] to serve others."

Ben and Dr. Thomas Bond worked together to start a hospital in 1751. It was named Pennsylvania Hospital. Ben was the hospital's second president.

Pennsylvania Hospital still remains today. It is one of the best hospitals in the country.

19

Schools and libraries

Ben loved books and learning. He wanted others to enjoy learning and reading, too.

But books were hard to get in the American **colonies**. Ben and his friends started the first **lending library**. The year was 1731. A lending library lets people borrow its books.

There were very few schools in the American colonies. Ben and his friends started a school in 1751. Today, that school is the University of Pennsylvania.

Here, Ben and his friends are opening their library.

fond	like a lot
lending library	library with books that can be borrowed and returned
public servant	person who works for the good of the public; a government worker

This is the University of Pennsylvania in early 1900.

Ben's words

"From a child I was **fond** of (liked) reading, and all the little money that came into my hands was ever laid out in books."

Ben began to work for the government. The government leads the country. He became a **public servant**. He worked for the good of the public. Ben held several government jobs.

Ben's public service started in the American colonies. But soon he would serve the American people from far across the ocean.

Diplomat

A **diplomat** is someone who gets along with others. Ben was a natural diplomat.

Ben went to the country of England. He told England that the American **colonies** wanted to rule themselves. The English would not agree to this.

The **American Revolutionary War** began in 1775. The American colonies fought against England. They fought to be **independent** from (not ruled by) England.

Ben told the government of England what the American colonies wanted.

American Revolutionary War war the American colonies fought with England from 1775 to 1783 in order to gain their independence

Then, the American colonies asked Ben to go to the country of France. The colonies needed France's help to win the war. Ben was an old man at this point. But he went to France. He convinced France to help the American colonies in the war with England.

The American colonies won the Revolutionary War. The colonies needed Ben again. Ben was happy and popular in France. He wanted to live in France for the rest of his life. Still, he came home to help his country.

Ben Franklin is wearing a fur hat in this picture.

Ben's words

"There never was a good war or a bad peace."

A Founding Father

Ben was an American leader. He helped write the **Declaration of Independence**. This was a special writing. It explained why the American colonies wanted to be free from England. Thomas Jefferson wrote most of the declaration. Ben and other members of the group helped him.

Ben did important work in France. He helped the French people to agree to a peace **treaty**. A treaty is an agreement between two or more countries. This treaty ended the **American Revolutionary War**.

Ben returned to the American colonies. Then, he helped write the U.S. **Constitution**. The Constitution was the plan for the new government of the United States of America. Ben was 81 years old. He had a lifetime of accomplishments behind him. He was very important to his country.

Here, Ben signs the Declaration of Independence.

Constitution	plan for the U.S. government
Declaration of Independence	writing sent to the king of England, in which Americans said they would no longer be ruled by England
treaty	agreement between two or more countries

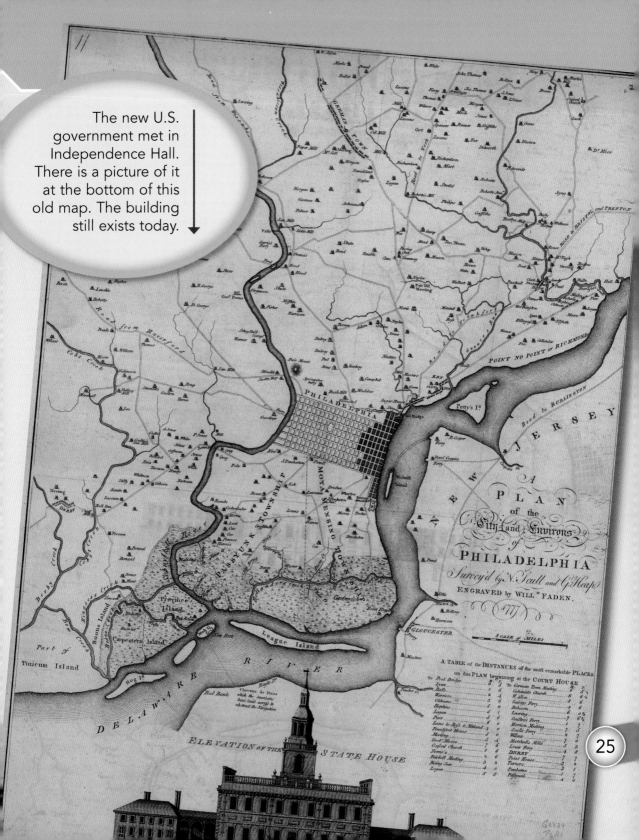

The new U.S. government met in Independence Hall. There is a picture of it at the bottom of this old map. The building still exists today.

Remembering Ben

Ben spent his final years in the city of Philadelphia. He enjoyed the company of family and friends. He died in 1790. He was 84 years old.

Twenty thousand people came to Ben's funeral. Ben was buried next to his wife, Deborah. Their graves are in Christ Church Cemetery in Philadelphia. The U.S. government said there would be 30 days of **mourning** for Ben. This was when people would feel and show sadness over Ben's death. In France many people wore black armbands to mourn Ben.

Ben gave much thought to what makes a good life. Like most people, he did not always do what he thought was "right." But he tried.

There is one more thing you should know about Ben. He was an excellent chess player. Ben thought that chess and life were much alike. They both take planning. You are better at both if you watch to see what others do. In chess and in life, you have to do your best to succeed.

Ben returned to Philadelphia in 1785. Here, his daughter, Sally, and her husband meet him.

Ben's words

"Wish not so much to live long as to live well."

There are many statues of Ben Franklin in the United States.

A Timeline of Ben's Life

1706   Born in Boston

1715   Last year of school

1718   Becomes an **apprentice** printer

1723   Runs away and gets a job as a printer in Philadelphia

1724   Travels to England; learns more about printing

1727   Helps to start the Junto Society

1729   Buys a newspaper

1730   Marries Deborah

1731   Starts a **lending library**

1732   Son, Frances Folger (Franky), is born

1732   Prints the first *Poor Richard's Almanac*

1735   Brother James dies

1736   Son Franky dies of **smallpox**

1737   Becomes **postmaster** (person in charge of the post office) in Philadelphia

1741   Designs the Franklin stove

1743   Daughter, Sally, is born

1744   Starts the American Philosophical Society

1745   Father dies

1746   Begins studying **electricity**

1752   Does experiment with kite

1753   Becomes **deputy** postmaster of North America

1762   Invents glass **armonica**

deputy	second in command
postmaster	person in charge of a post office
slavery	system in which people own other people

1774 Wife, Deborah, dies while Ben is in England

1775 Elected to represent Pennsylvania in the government of the American **colonies**

1775 Elected to be postmaster general for the American colonies

1776 Is one of five men who write the **Declaration of Independence**

1776 Goes to France as a **diplomat**

1783 Signs peace **treaty**

1784 Invents **bifocal** eyeglasses

1785 Elected president of the Pennsylvania government

1787 Signs the U.S. **Constitution**

1789 Writes about and works to stop **slavery** (practice of owning other people)

1790 Dies on April 17

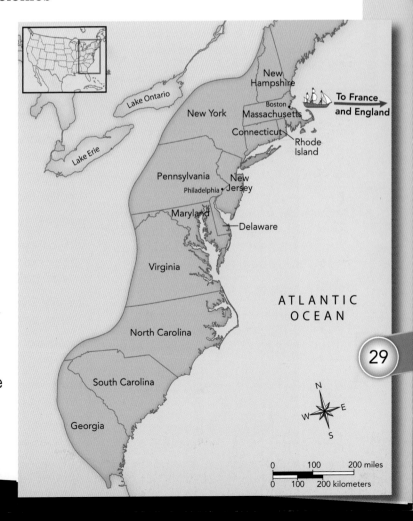

Glossary

almanac book printed once a year that includes a calendar and weather forecasts

American Revolutionary War war the American colonies fought with England from 1775 to 1783 in order to gain their independence

apprentice person who is learning a job

armonica instrument played by touching the edges of spinning glass bowls with wet fingers

article short writing such as those printed in newspapers

bifocals eyeglasses that have two parts. One part is for seeing things close. The other part is for seeing things far away.

chimney part of a fireplace that lets smoke out of a house

colony land belonging to or under the control of a nation that is far away

Constitution plan for the U.S. government

Declaration of Independence writing sent to the king of England, in which Americans said they would no longer be ruled by England

deputy second in command

diplomat person who is good at dealing with other people. Diplomats often work for the government of a country.

electricity type of energy. Energy makes things work.

forecast to tell what will happen at a later date (such as the weather)

independent not ruled by others; responsible for oneself

issue what is important at the time, such as wars or public needs

lending library library with books that can be borrowed and returned

lens clear part of eyeglasses that is looked through

lightning flashes of light seen during a storm

mourning feeling or showing sadness over someone's death

opportunity chance

philosopher person known for ideas and thinking

postmaster person in charge of a post office

printing press machine used to print newspapers and signs

public servant person who works for the good of the public; a government worker

resolve decide

seldom not often

service group that works for the needs of the public, such as a police department

slavery system in which people own other people

smallpox serious illness that can cause death

treaty agreement between two or more countries

volunteer person who provides a service without being paid

Want to Know More?

Books to read

- Aliki. *The Many Lives of Benjamin Franklin*. New York: Simon and Schuster, 1988.

- Giblin, James Cross. *The Amazing Life of Benjamin Franklin*. New York: Scholastic, 2006.

- Sherrow, Victoria. *Benjamin Franklin*. Minneapolis, MN: Lerner, 2002.

Websites

- **Ben's Guide to U.S. Government for Kids**
  http://bensguide.gpo.gov/benfranklin/index.html

- **Play the Armonica**
  http://www.fi.edu/franklin/musician/virtualarmonica.html

Places to visit

- **Independence Hall**
  Independence NHP
  143 S. Third Street
  Philadelphia, PA 19106
  Free Tickets are available the morning of your visit at the Independence Visitor Center.
  For Philadelphia Visitor Information: (215) 965-7676

Read ***Designing America: The Constitutional Convention*** to find out what went on behind the closed doors of Independence Hall.

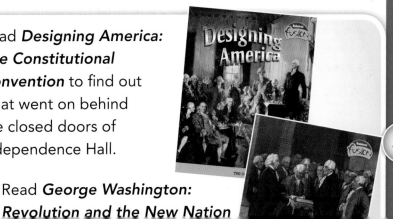

Read ***George Washington: Revolution and the New Nation***

Index